Table of Contents

Introduction

*I have sworn upon the altar of
God eternal hostility against
every form of tyranny over the
mind of man.*

Thomas Jefferson, born in Virginia in 1743, lived in an age of revolution and emerging democracy. Through his ideas and active service as a statesman, he more than any other American placed his stamp on that democratic experiment, the United States of America.

After attending William and Mary College in Williamsburg, Virginia and studying law under George Wythe who later became first professor of law at the College, Jefferson was elected in 1769 to the Virginia House of Burgesses where he served until 1776. He attended the Continental Congress in Philadelphia in 1775-76 and was from 1776-79 a member of the Virginia House of Delegates. He served one term as Governor of Virginia (and was almost captured by the British as they drove through Charlottesville and his

Thomas Jefferson
★His Life and Words★

Edited by Nick Beilenson
Illustrated by Rachael A. Peden

PETER PAUPER PRESS, INC.
WHITE PLAINS • NEW YORK

mountaintop estate at Monticello). Jefferson served as Minister to France from 1785-89 and as Secretary of State under President Washington from 1790-93.

Jefferson ran for president in 1796 against John Adams. He received the second highest vote in the electoral balloting and, in accordance with the Constitution as then written, was designated vice-president. In 1800 he again ran for president, as standard-bearer of the Republican (now Democratic) Party, defeating the Federalist Adams handily. After political maneuvering brought on by the fact that Jefferson and his running mate Burr received the same number of votes in the electoral college, he was elected by the House of Representatives in 1801 as third president of the United States. Jefferson served two terms as president and then retired in 1809 to his beloved Monticello. During his retirement, he oversaw his estate, kept up a monumental correspondence (he wrote over 15,000 letters during his lifetime), and founded the University of Virginia at nearby Charlottesville. He died on July 4, 1826 at the age of 83.

Jefferson played a crucial role in the Revolutionary Era not only as statesman and politician but through his seminal writings, political documents firmly based on the philosophical doctrine of the law of nature. His 1774 *Summary View of the Rights of British America,* which declared that "the British parliament has no right to exercise authority over us," brought Jefferson to the attention of two continents. Two years later, he drafted the Declaration of Independence, and in 1777 he drafted the Virginia Bill for Establishing Religious Freedom which called for political equality for all citizens regardless of their religion or lack of it.

Jefferson was not only a statesman and politician. He was a lawyer, educator, mathematician, surveyor, philosopher, scientist, architect, geographer, philologist, and musician. President John F. Kennedy truly had reason to say to a group of Nobel Laureates: "I think that this is the most extraordinary collection of talent, of human knowledge, that has ever gathered together at the White House, with the possible exception of when Thomas Jefferson dined alone."

Jefferson married Martha Wayles Skelton, the daughter of a wealthy Virginia landowner, in 1772. Nine months later their daughter Martha was born, and Mary was born in 1778.

Of the Jeffersons' six children, only Martha and Mary grew to maturity, and only Martha survived her father. Jefferson's wife Martha died in 1782, having been in poor health since the birth of their sixth child. Jefferson, a widower at age 39, never remarried.

* * * * *

In this slim book, Thomas Jefferson speaks for himself, in words that have retained their force, eloquence, and relevance to the present day. The selections that follow are meant, in a small space, to introduce the reader to Jefferson's major public writings and addresses, to his political philosophy, and to as many facets of the man, both public and private, as is possible. The source of each quotation, whenever it would be of interest to the general reader, is placed in brackets at the end of the selection.

N.B.

Jefferson Memorial
Washington, D.C.

The Jefferson Memorial

The words that follow, reflecting Thomas Jefferson's most important principles, are inscribed on four panels on the walls of the Jefferson Memorial in Washington, D.C.

First Panel: Declaration of Independence

We hold these truths to be self-evident: that all men are created equal, that they are endowed by their Creator with certain inalienable rights, among these are life, liberty and the pursuit of happiness, that to secure these rights governments are instituted among men. We ... solemnly publish and declare, that these colonies are and of right ought to be free and independent states ... And for the support of this declaration, with a firm reliance on the protection of divine providence, we mutually pledge our lives, our fortunes, and our sacred honour.

Second Panel: Religious Freedom

Almighty God hath created the mind free. All attempts to influence it by temporal punishments or burthens ... are a departure from the plan of the Holy Author of our religion ... No man shall be compelled to frequent or support any religious worship or ministry or shall otherwise suffer on account of his religious opinions or belief, but all men shall be free to profess and by argument to maintain, their opinions in matters of religion. I know but one code of morality for men whether acting singly or collectively.

Third Panel: Slavery/Education

God who gave us life gave us liberty. Can the liberties of a nation be secure when we have removed a conviction that these liberties are the gift of God? Indeed I tremble for my country when I reflect that God is just, that his justice cannot sleep forever. Commerce between master and slave is despotism. Nothing is more certainly written in the book of fate than that these people are to be free. Establish the law for educating the common people. This it is the business of the state to effect and on a general plan.

Fourth Panel: Constitution and Laws

I am not an advocate for frequent changes in laws and constitutions, but laws and institutions must go hand in hand with the progress of the human mind. As that becomes more developed, more enlightened, as new discoveries are made, new truths discovered and manners and opinions change, with the change of circumstances, institutions must advance also to keep pace with the times. We might as well require a man to wear still the coat which fitted him when a boy as civilized society to remain ever under the regimen of their barbarous ancestors.

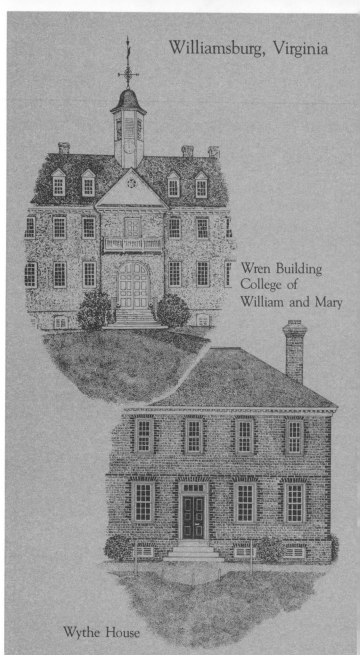

Williamsburg, Virginia

Wren Building
College of
William and Mary

Wythe House

Jefferson the Democrat

Jefferson, the patrician landowner, lived in and reflected an age of revolution and democracy. He believed men derive their political rights from the law of nature, against which royal edicts and laws of Parliament must give way. Life and liberty are inseparable. If blood must be shed to defend these rights, so be it. The majority should rule, but loses legitimacy if it fails to respect the rights of the minority. Government should control its citizenry to the minimum possible extent. An educated electorate and a free press are necessary to the successful workings of democracy. Summarizing Jefferson's commitment to democracy are these excerpts from his draft of the Declaration of Independence:

★ We hold these truths to be self evident: that all men are created equal; that they are endowed by their Creator with inherent and inalienable rights; that among these are life, liberty, and the pursuit of happiness; that to

13

secure these rights, governments are instituted among men, deriving their just powers from the consent of the governed; that whenever any form of government becomes destructive of these ends, it is the right of the people to alter or to abolish it, and to institute new government, laying its foundation on such principles, and organizing its power in such form, as to them shall seem most likely to effect their safety and happiness. Prudence, indeed, will dictate that governments long established should not be changed for light and transient causes . . .

(The King) has dissolved representative houses repeatedly . . .

He has kept among us in times of peace standing armies . . .

He has waged cruel war against human nature itself, violating its most sacred rights of life and liberty in the persons of a distant people who never offended him, captivating and carrying them into slavery in another hemisphere, or to incur miserable death in their transportation hither. . . .

We therefore . . . reject and renounce all allegiance and subjection to the kings of Great Britain . . . we utterly dissolve all political connection . . . and finally we do assert and declare these colonies to be free and independent states . . . [June, 1776]

★ [These grievances] we have thus laid before his majesty with that freedom of language and sentiment which becomes a free people . . . kings are the servants, not the proprietors of the people. . . . The god who gave us life, gave us liberty at the same time: the hand of force may destroy, but cannot disjoin them. [A SUMMARY VIEW OF THE RIGHTS OF BRITISH AMERICA, 1774]

★ Sensible, however, of the importance of unanimity among our constituents [in Virginia on the issue of independence], although we often wished to have gone faster, we slackened our pace, that our less ardent colleagues might keep up with us; and they, on their part, differing nothing from us in principle, quickened their gait somewhat beyond that which their prudence might of itself have advised, and thus consolidated the phalanx which breasted the power of Britain. By this harmony of the bold with the cautious, we advanced our constituents in undivided mass, and with fewer ex-

15

amples of separation than, perhaps, existed in any other part of the Union.

★ I consider the people who constitute a society or nation as the source of all authority in that nation. [OPINION ON THE FRENCH TREATIES, 1793]

★ What signify a few lives lost in a century or two? The tree of liberty must be refreshed from time to time with the blood of patriots & tyrants. It is it's natural manure. [1787 LETTER FROM PARIS TO WILLIAM S. SMITH]

★ All Europe, Russia excepted, has caught the spirit, and all will attain representative government, more or less perfect. . . . To attain all this however rivers of blood must yet flow, and years of desolation pass over. [1823 LETTER TO JOHN ADAMS]

★ The ball of liberty is now so well in motion that it will roll round the globe. [1795 LETTER TO TENCH COXE]

★ All, too, will bear in mind this sacred principle, that though the will of the majority is in all cases to prevail, that will, to be rightful, must be reasonable; that the minority possess their equal rights, which equal laws must protect, and to violate which would be oppression. . . .

. . . Equal and exact justice to all men, of whatever state or persuasion, religious or political; peace, commerce, and honest friendship, with all nations—entangling alliances with none . . . the supremacy of the civil over the military authority . . . freedom of religion; freedom of the press; freedom of person under the protection of the *habeas corpus;* and trial by juries impartially selected—these principles . . . guided our steps through an age of revolution and reformation. [FIRST INAUGURAL ADDRESS, 1801]

★ A leader may offer, but not impose himself, nor be imposed on (the people).

★ The disease of liberty is catching. [1820 LETTER TO LAFAYETTE]

★ A wise and frugal government, which shall restrain men from injuring one another, shall leave them otherwise free to regulate their own pursuits of industry and improvement, and shall not take from the mouth of labor the bread it has earned.

★ If we can prevent the Government from wasting the labors of the people, under the pretense of taking care of them, they must become happy.

★ The force of public opinion cannot be resisted when permitted freely to be expressed. Whenever the people are well informed, they can be trusted with their own Government.

★ In every government on earth is some trace of human weakness, some germ of corruption and degeneracy, which cunning will discover, and wickedness insensibly open, cultivate, and improve. Every government degenerates when trusted to the rulers of the people alone. The people themselves are its only safe depositories. And to render even them safe their minds must be improved to a certain degree. [NOTES ON THE STATE OF VIRGINIA, 1781]

★ We are not to expect to be translated from despotism to liberty in a featherbed. [1790 LETTER TO LAFAYETTE]

★ Were it left to me to decide whether we should have a government without newspapers, or newspapers without government, I should not hesitate a moment to prefer the latter. But I should mean that every man . . . be capable of reading them. [1787 LETTER TO EDWARD CARRINGTON]

★ The Constitution of the United States is the result of the collected wisdom of our country. [1801 LETTER TO AMOS MARSH]

★ With all the imperfections of our present government, it is without comparison the best existing or that ever did exist.

19

Washington, D.C.

The Capitol

The White House

Jefferson on Public Policy

Jefferson believed in a government of laws and not of men, of separation of powers, and in states' rights. Government should be small, taxes invisible and the public debt paid. While praising a free press, he damned its "licentiousness." He favored the principles that later became known as the Monroe Doctrine. Naturalization should be eased. The Constitution should be amended when necessary. Cuba would be a welcome addition to the United States.

★ It would be a dangerous delusion were a confidence in the men of our choice to silence our fears for the safety of our rights: that confidence is everywhere the parent of despotism—free government is founded on jealousy, and not in confidence; it is jealousy and not confidence which prescribes limited constitutions ... In questions of power, then, let no more be heard of confidence in man, but bind him down from mischief by the chains of the Constitution. [KENTUCKY RESOLUTIONS, 1798]

★ (A Bill of Rights) would help create a national sentiment to 'counteract the impulses of interest and passion' of popular majorities and provide a rallying point against a usurping government.

★ The Legislative, Executive and Judiciary offices shall be kept for ever separate, & no person exercising the one shall be capable of appointment to the others, or to either of them. . . .

Every person of full age neither owning nor having owned [50] acres of land, shall be entitled to an appropriation of [50] acres or to so much as shall make up (a full 50 acres) . . . [DRAFT CONSTITUTION FOR VIRGINIA, 1776]

★ *Resolved,* That the several States composing the United States of America; are not united on the principle of unlimited submission to their General Government; but that, by a compact under the style and title of a Constitution for the United States, and of amendments thereto, they constituted a General Government for special purposes,—delegated to that government certain definite powers, reserving, each State to itself, the residuary mass of right to their own self-government; and that whensoever the General Government assumes undelegated powers, its acts are unauthoritative, void, and of no force . . . [KENTUCKY RESOLUTIONS}

★ Unless the President's mind on a view of everything which is urged for and against this bill [for the establishment of a National Bank], is tolerably clear that it is unauthorised by the Constitution; if the pro and the con hang so even as to balance his judgment, a just respect for the wisdom of the legislature would naturally decide the balance in favor of their opinion. It is chiefly for cases where they are clearly misled by error, ambition, or interest, that the Constitution has placed a check in the negative of the President. [OPINION ON THE CONSTITUTIONALITY OF A NATIONAL BANK, 1791]

★ The remaining revenue on the consumption of foreign articles, is paid cheerfully by those who can afford to add foreign luxuries to domestic comforts, being collected on our seaboards and frontiers only, and incorporated with the transactions of our mercantile citizens, it may be the pleasure and pride of an American to ask, what farmer, what mechanic, what laborer, ever sees a tax-gatherer of the United States? [SECOND INAUGURAL ADDRESS, 1805]

★ During this course of administration, and in order to disturb it, the artillery of the press has been levelled against us, charged with whatsoever its licentiousness could devise or dare. These abuses of an institution so important to freedom and science, are deeply to be regretted, inasmuch as they tend to lessen its usefulness, and to sap its safety . . .

. . . since truth and reason have maintained their ground against false opinions in league with false facts, the press, confined to truth, needs no other legal restraint; the public judgment will correct false reasonings and opinions, on a full hearing of all parties . . . [SECOND INAUGURAL ADDRESS]

24

★ Newspapers serve to carry off noxious vapors and smoke. [1802 LETTER TO TADEUSZ KOSCIUSKO]

★ I place economy among the first and most important virtues, and public debt as the greatest of the dangers to be feared. [1816 LETTER TO WILLIAM PLUMER]

★ We must make our election between *economy and liberty, or profusion and servitude.* [1816 LETTER TO SAMUEL KERCHEVAL]

★ When we consider that this government is charged with the external and mutual relations only of these states; that the states themselves have principal care of our persons, our property, and our reputation, constituting the great field of human concerns, we may well doubt whether our organization is not too complicated, too expensive; whether offices and officers have not been multiplied unnecessarily, and sometimes injuriously to the service they were meant to promote. [FIRST ANNUAL MESSAGE TO CONGRESS, 1801]

★ Great Britain is the nation which can do us the most harm of any one, or all on earth; and with her on our side we need not fear the whole world. [1823 LETTER TO PRESIDENT JAMES MONROE]

★ Our first and fundamental maxim should be, never to entangle ourselves in the broils of Europe. Our second, never to suffer Europe to intermeddle with cis-Atlantic affairs. America, North and South, has a set of interests distinct from those of Europe, and peculiarly her own. She should therefore have a system of her own, separate and apart from that of Europe. [THE MONROE DOCTRINE— 1823 LETTER TO PRESIDENT JAMES MONROE]

★ I cannot omit recommending a revisal of the laws on the subject of naturalization. . . . shall we refuse the unhappy fugitives from distress that hospitality which the savages of the wilderness extended to our fathers arriving in this land? Shall oppressed humanity find no asylum on this globe? [FIRST ANNUAL MESSAGE TO CONGRESS]

★ Do we wish to acquire to our own confederacy any one or more of the Spanish provinces? I candidly confess, that I have ever looked on Cuba as the most interesting addition which could ever be made to our system of States. [1823 LETTER TO PRESIDENT JAMES MONROE]

★ Some men look at constitutions with sanctimonious reverence, and deem them like the ark of the covenant, too sacred to be touched. They ascribe to the men of the preceding age a wisdom more than human, and suppose what they did to be beyond amendment. I knew that age well; I belonged to it, and labored with it. . . . But I know also, that laws and institutions must go hand in hand with the progress of the human mind. As that becomes more developed, more enlightened, as new discoveries are made, new truths disclosed, and manners and opinions change with the change of circumstances, institutions must advance also, and keep pace with the times. [1816 LETTER TO SAMUEL KERCHEVAL]

Virginia State Capitol
Richmond, Virginia

Jefferson on Religion and Moral Law

Jefferson considered himself a Christian. Religious belief was between man's conscience and his God, and all beliefs should be tolerated. He had little use for much of the clergy. Outside the edifice of government should stand a "wall" between it and religion. Jefferson's most eloquent statement of political separation between church and state is embodied in his Bill for Establishing Religious Freedom.

★ I am a *real Christian,* that is to say, a disciple of the doctrines of Jesus, very different from the Platonists, who call *me* infidel and *themselves* Christians and preachers of the gospel, while they draw all their characteristic dogmas from what its author never said nor saw. They have compounded from the heathen mysteries a system beyond the comprehension of man, of which (Jesus), were he to return on earth, would not recognize one feature. [1816 Letter to Charles Thomson]

★ The doctrines of Jesus are simple, and tend all to the happiness of man. 1. That there is only one God, and he all perfect. 2. That there is a future state of rewards and punishments. 3. That to love God with all thy heart and thy neighbor as thyself, is the sum of religion. [1822 LETTER TO DR. BENJAMIN WATERHOUSE]

★ I say, that this free exercise of reason is all I ask for the vindication of the character of Jesus. We find in the writings of his biographers matter of two distinct descriptions. First, a groundwork of vulgar ignorance, of things impossible, of superstitions, fanaticisms and fabrications. Intermixed with these, again, are sublime ideas of the Supreme Being, aphorisms and precepts of the purest morality and benevolence, sanctioned by a life of humility, innocence and simplicity of manners, neglect of riches, absence of worldly ambition and honors, with an eloquence and persuasiveness which have not been surpassed. These could not be inventions of the groveling authors who relate them. They are far beyond the powers of their feeble minds. They show that there was a character, the subject of their history, whose splendid conceptions were above all suspicion of being interpolations from their hands. [1820 LETTER TO WILLIAM SHORT]

★ You will next read the new testament. It is the history of a personage called Jesus. Keep in your eye the opposite pretensions. 1. Of those who say he was begotten by god, born of a virgin, suspended and reversed the laws of nature at will, and ascended bodily into heaven: and 2. of those who say he was a man, of illegitimate birth, of a benevolent heart, enthusiastic mind, who set out without pretensions to divinity, ended in believing them, and was punished capitally for sedition . . . If (your inquiry) ends in a belief that there is no god, you will find incitements to virtue in the comfort and pleasantness you feel in it's exercise, and the love of others which it will procure you. If you find reason to believe there is a god, a consciousness that you are acting under his eye, and that he approves you, will be a vast additional incitement. If that there be a future state, the hope of a happy existence in that increases the appetite to deserve it; if that Jesus was also a god, you will be comforted by a belief of his aid and love. [1787 LETTER TO NEPHEW PETER CARR]

★ I have ever thought religion a concern purely between our God and our consciences, for which we were accountable to him, and not to the priests. I never told my own religion, nor scrutinized that of another. I never attempted to make a convert, nor wished to change another's creed. I have ever judged of the religion of others by their lives . . . For it is in our lives, and not from our words, that our religion must be read. [1816 LETTER TO MRS. SAMUEL H. SMITH]

★ My opinion is that there would never have been an infidel, if there had never been a priest. The artificial structures they have built on the purest of all moral systems, for the purpose of deriving from it pence and power, revolts those who think for themselves, and who read in that system only what is really there. [1816 LETTER TO MRS. SAMUEL H. SMITH]

★ Compulsion in religion is distinguished peculiarly from compulsion in every other thing. I may grow rich by an act I am compelled to follow, I may recover health by medicines I am compelled to take against my own judgment, but I cannot be saved by a worship I disbelieve and abhor.

★ (I regret that the Jewish sect) parent and basis of all those of Christendom (has been singled out by Christians) for a persecution and oppression which proved they have profited nothing from the benevolent doctrines of him whom they profess to make the model of their principles and practice. [1820 LETTER TO JOSEPH MARX]

★ Believing with you that religion is a matter that lies solely between man and his God, that he owes account to none other for his faith or his worship, that the legislative powers of government reach actions only, and not opinions, I contemplate with sovereign reverence that act of the whole American people which declared that their legislature should "make no law respecting an establishment of religion, or prohibiting the free exercise thereof," thus building a wall of separation between Church and State. [STATEMENT AS PRESIDENT TO CONNECTICUT BAPTISTS, 1802]

★ Well aware that the opinions and belief of men depend not on their own will, but follow involuntarily the evidence proposed to their minds; that Almighty God hath created the mind free, and manifested his supreme will that free it shall remain by making it altogether insusceptible of restraint; . . . that our civil rights have no dependance on our religious opinions, any more than our opinions in physics and geometry; . . . that the opinions of men are not the object of civil government, nor under its jurisdiction; that to suffer the civil magistrate to intrude his powers into the field of opinion and to restrain the profession or propagation of principles on supposition of their ill tendency is a dangerous falacy, which at once destroys all religious liberty . . . that it is time enough for the rightful purposes of civil government for its officers to interfere when principles break out into overt acts against peace and good order; and finally, that

truth is great and will prevail if left to herself;
. . .

We, the General Assembly of Virginia do enact that no man shall be compelled to frequent or support any religious worship, place, or ministry whatsoever, nor shall be enforced, restrained, molested, or burthened in his body or goods, nor shall otherwise suffer, on account of his religious opinions or belief; but that all men shall be free to profess, and by argument to maintain, their opinions in matters of religion, and that the same shall in no wise diminish, enlarge, or affect their civil capacities. [JEFFERSON'S 1777 DRAFT BILL FOR ESTABLISHING RELIGIOUS FREEDOM]

★ In matters of religion, I have considered that its free exercise is placed by the constitution independent of the powers of the general government. I have therefore undertaken, on no occasion, to prescribe the religious exercises suited to it; but have left them, as the constitution found them, under the direction and discipline of State or Church authorities acknowledged by the several religious societies. [SECOND INAUGURAL ADDRESS, 1805]

Monticello
Charlottesville, Virginia

Jefferson on Slaves, Women, Indians

Jefferson was unalterably opposed to continuation of the slave trade. He believed that slavery irreparably damaged both black and white, and favored emancipation. Nevertheless, he opposed miscegenation, and expressed doubt as to the intellectual abilities of the Negro. He remained the owner of slaves throughout his lifetime, freeing a small minority at his death. As to women, Jefferson was clear that their place was in the home, not in politics. Interestingly, Jefferson had great respect for Virginia's Indians and their political system.

★ No person hereafter coming into this country shall be held within the same in slavery under any pretext whatever. [DRAFT CONSTITUTION FOR VIRGINIA, 1776]

★ In the very first session held under the republican government [in Virginia], the assembly passed a law for the perpetual prohibition of the importation of slaves. This will in some measure stop the increase of this great political and moral evil, while the minds of our citizens may be ripening for a complete emancipation of human nature. [NOTES ON THE STATE OF VIRGINIA, 1781]

★ The whole commerce between master and slave is a perpetual exercise of the most boisterous passions, the most unremitting despotism on the one part, and degrading submissions on the other. Our children see this, and learn to imitate it; for man is an imitative animal. This quality is the germ of all education in him. . . . The parent storms, the child looks on, catches the lineaments of wrath, puts on the same airs in the circle of smaller slaves, gives a loose to his worst of passions, and thus nursed, educated, and daily exercised in tyranny, cannot but be stamped by it with odious peculiarities. . . . And with what execration should the stateman be loaded, who permitting one half the citizens thus to trample on the rights of the other, transforms those into despots, and these into enemies . . . [NOTES ON THE STATE OF VIRGINIA]

★ The love of justice and the love of country plead equally the cause of these people, and it is a moral reproach to us that they should have pleaded it so long in vain, and should have produced not a single effort . . . to relieve them & ourselves from our present condition of moral & political reprobation. . . . few minds have yet doubted but that they were as legitimate subjects of property as their horses and cattle.

. . . Their amalgamation with any other color produces a degradation to which no lover of his country, no lover of excellence in the human character can innocently consent. [1814 LETTER TO EDWARD COLES]

★ The improvement of the blacks in body and mind, in the first instance of their mixture with the whites, has been observed by every one, and proves that their inferiority is not the effect merely of their condition of life. [NOTES ON THE STATE OF VIRGINIA]

★ Never yet could I find that a black had uttered a thought above the level of plain narration; never see even an elementary trait of painting or sculpture. In music they are more generally gifted than the whites with accurate ears for tune and time . . . Whether they will be equal to the composition of a more extensive run of melody, or of complicated harmony, is yet to be proved. Misery is often the parent of the most affecting touches in poetry.—Among the blacks is misery enough, God knows, but no poetry. (NOTES ON THE STATE OF VIRGINIA)

★ Be assured that no person living wishes more sincerely than I do, to see a complete refutation of the doubts I have myself entertained and expressed on the grade of understanding allotted to (blacks) by nature, and to find that in this respect they are on a par with ourselves. My doubts were the result of personal observation on the limited sphere of my own State, where the opportunities for the development of their genius were not favorable, and those of exercising it still less so. I expressed them therefore with great hesitation; but whatever be their degree of talent it is no measure of their rights. Because Sir Isaac Newton was superior to others in understanding, he was not therefore lord of the person or property of others. On this subject they are gaining daily in the opinion of nations, and hopeful advances are making towards their reestablishment on an equal footing with the other colors of the human family. [1809 LETTER TO HENRI GREGOIRE]

★ I consider a [slave] woman who brings a child every two years as more profitable than the best man of the farm.

★ Were our State a pure democracy . . . there would yet be excluded from their deliberations . . . women who, to prevent deprivation of morals and ambiguity of issue, could not mix promiscuously in the public meetings of men. [1816 LETTER TO SAMUEL KERCHEVAL]

★ The tender breasts of ladies were not formed for political convulsion.

★ The appointment of a woman to office is an innovation for which the public is not prepared, nor am I. [1807 LETTER TO ALBERT GALLATIN]

★ (Dancing) is a necessary accomplishment, therefore, although of short use, for the French rule is wise, that no lady dances after marriage. This is founded in solid physical reasons, gestation and nursing leaving little time to a married lady when this exercise can be either safe or innocent. [1818 LETTER TO NATHANIEL BURWELL]

★ I do love this [French] *people* with all my heart, and think that with better religion and a better form of government and their present governors their condition and country would be most enviable. I pray you to observe that I have used the term *people* and that this is a noun of the masculine as well as feminine gender. [1785 LETTER TO ABIGAIL ADAMS]

★ (Indians have) never submitted themselves to any laws, any coercive power, any shadow of government. Their only controuls are their manners, and that moral sense of right and wrong, which, like the sense of tasting and feeling, in every man makes a part of his nature. An offence against these is punished by contempt, by exclusion from society, or, where the case is serious, as that of murder, by the individuals whom it concerns. Imperfect as this species of coercion may seem, crimes are very rare among them . . . [NOTES ON THE STATE OF VIRGINIA]

★ An inhuman practice once prevailed in this country of making slaves of the Indians. . . . With them it is disgraceful to be hairy on the body. They say it likens them to hogs. They therefore pluck the hair as fast as it appears. . . . The principles of their society forbidding all compulsion, they are to be led to duty and to enterprise by personal influence and persuasion. Hence eloquence in council, bravery and address in war, become the foundations of all consequence with them. . . . Of their bravery and address in war we have multiplied proofs, because we have been the subjects on which they were exercised. [NOTES ON THE STATE OF VIRGINIA]

The Garden Pavilion
at Monticello

Jefferson the Man

In his letters Jefferson gossiped, grieved, praised marriage, and defined happiness. He loved music. He had a strong moral sense. He was free with advice to his children and grandchildren. He felt himself to be a private man, a scientist, who had been led by events into public service. As Jefferson served out his second term, he expressed fatigue and the desire to return to private life.

★ When I recollect that at 14. years of age, the whole care and direction of my self was thrown on my self entirely, without a relation or friend qualified to advise or guide me, and recollect the various sorts of bad company with which I associated from time to time, I am astonished I did not turn off with some of them, and become as worthless to society as they were. I had the good fortune to become acquainted very early with some characters of very high standing, and to feel the incessant wish that I could even become what they were. [1808 LETTER TO GRANDSON THOMAS JEFFERSON RANDOLPH]

★ If there is any news stirring in town or country, such as deaths, courtships, or marriages, in the circle of my acquaintance, let me know it. Remember me affectionately to all the young ladies of my acquaintance, particularly the Miss Burwells, and Miss Potters, and tell them that though that heavy earthly part of me, my body, be absent, the better half of me, my soul, is ever with them; and that my best wishes shall ever attend them. [1762 LETTER TO JOHN PAGE]

★ Harmony in the married state is the very first object to be aimed at. The happiness of the domestic fireside is the first boon of Heaven.

★ I . . . lost the cherished companion of my life, in whose affections, unabated on both sides, I had lived the last ten years in unchequered happiness. [AUTOBIOGRAPHY, 1821]

★ Health is the first requisite after morality. [1787 LETTER TO PETER CARR]

★ I have ever found time and silence the only medicine [for loss of a loved one], and these but assuage, they never can suppress, the deep-drawn sigh which recollection for ever brings up, until recollection and life are extinguished together. [1813 LETTER TO JOHN ADAMS]

★ Give up money, give up fame, give up science, give [up] the earth itself and all it contains, rather than do an immoral act. . . . Whenever you are to do a thing, though it can never be known but to yourself, ask yourself how you would act were all the world looking at you, and act accordingly. . . . There is no vice so mean, so pitiful, so contemptible; and he who permits himself to tell a lie once, finds it much easier to do it a second and third time, till at length it becomes habitual; he tells lies without attending to it, and truths without the world's believing him. [1785 LETTER TO PETER CARR]

★ I find as I grow older that I love those most whom I loved first.

★ It is your future happiness which interests me, and nothing can contribute more to it (moral rectitude always excepted) than the contracting a habit of industry and activity. Of all the cankers of human happiness nothing corrodes with so silent, yet so baneful a tooth, as indolence. Body and mind, both unemployed, our being becomes a burden, and every object about us loathesome, even the dearest. Idleness begets ennui, ennui the hypochondria, and that a diseased body. No laborious person was ever yet hysterical. Exercise and application produce order in our affairs, health of body, cheerfulness of mind, and these make us precious to our friends. . . . . [if] you catch yourself in idleness, start from it as you would from the precipice of a gulf. You are not, however, to consider yourself as unemployed while taking exercise. This is necessary for your health. [1787 LETTER TO MARTHA JEFFERSON, AT AGE 15]

★ With respect to the distribution of your time the following is what I should approve.
from 8. to 10 o'clock practise music.
from 10. to 1. dance one day and draw another
from 1. to 2. draw on the day you dance, and

write a letter the next day.
from 3. to 4. read French
from 4. to 5. exercise yourself in music.
from 5. till bedtime read English, write &c.
. . . If you love me then, strive to be good under every situation and to all living creatures, and to acquire those accomplishments which I have put in your power . . . [1783 LETTER TO DAUGHTER MARTHA, AGE 11!]

★ The glow of one warm thought is to me worth more than money.

★ Be a listener only, keep within yourself, and endeavor to establish with yourself the habit of silence, especially in politics. [1808 LETTER TO GRANDSON THOMAS JEFFERSON RANDOLPH]

★ If there is a gratification which I envy any people in this world it is to [Italy] its music. This is the favorite passion of my soul, and fortune has cast my lot in a country where it is in a state of deplorable barbarism. [1787 LETTER TO GIOVANNI FABBRONI]

★ Man was destined for society. His morality, therefore, was to be formed to this object. He was endowed with a sense of right and wrong, merely relative to this. This sense is as much a part of his nature as his sense of hearing, seeing, feeling; it is the true foundation of morality . . . It may be strengthened by exercise . . . This sense is submitted in some degree to the guidance of reason; but it is a small stock which is required for this . . . State a moral case to a ploughman and a professor. The former will decide it as well, and often better than the latter, because he has not yet been led astray by artificial rules . . . [1787 LETTER TO PETER CARR FROM PARIS]

★ The whole of my life has been a war with my natural taste, feelings and wishes; domestic life and literary pursuits were my first and my latest inclinations—circumstances and not my desires led me to the path I have trod . . .

★ I have tired you, my friend, with a long letter. But your tedium will end in a few lines more. Mine has yet two years to endure. I am tired of an office [the presidency] where I can do no more good than many others, who would be glad to be employed in it. To myself, personally, it brings nothing but unceasing drudgery & daily loss of friends. [1807 LETTER TO JOHN DICKINSON]

★ Within a few days I retire to my family, my books and farms; and having gained the harbor myself, I shall look on my friends still buffeting the storm, with anxiety indeed, but not with envy. Never did a prisoner, released from his chains, feel such relief as I shall on shaking off the shackles of power. Nature intended me for the tranquil pursuits of science, by rendering them my supreme delight. But the enormities of the times in which I have lived, have forced me to take a part in resisting them, and to commit myself on the boisterous ocean of political passions. [1809 LETTER TO P.S. DUPONT DE NEMOURS]

★ Take care of me when dead . . . [1826 LETTER TO JAMES MADISON]

The Rotunda
University of Virginia

Jefferson the Observer

Jefferson held trenchant and sometimes witty views on most all subjects, including youth and age, books and printing, disputation, the American character, travel, lawyers, George Washington, and Great Britain.

★ It is while we are young that the habit of industry is formed. If not then, it never is afterwards. The fortune of our lives, therefore, depends on employing well the short period of youth.

★ The boys of the rising generation are to be the men of the next, and the sole guardian of the principles we deliver over to them.

★ It is objected . . . that he is 77 years of age [too old for public office]; but at a much more advanced age, our Franklin was the ornament of human nature. He may not be able to perform, in person, all the details of his office; but if he gives us the benefit of his understanding, his integrity, his watchfulness, and takes care that all the details are well performed by himself or his necessary assistants, all public purposes will be answered. [1801 LETTER TO ELIAS SHIPMAN AND OTHERS, A COMMITTEE OF THE MERCHANTS OF NEW HAVEN]

★ Whenever a man has cast a longing eye on them [public offices], a rottenness begins in his conduct. [1799 LETTER TO TENCH COXE]

★ No duty the Executive had to perform was so trying as to put the right man in the right place.

★ The light which has been shed on mankind by the art of printing has eminently changed the condition of the world. [1823 LETTER TO JOHN ADAMS]

★ Books constitute capital. A library book lasts as long as a house, for hundreds of years. It is not an article of mere consumption but fairly of capital, and often in the case of professional men, setting out in life, it is their only capital. [1821 LETTER TO JAMES MADISON]

★ I have often thought that nothing would do more extensive good at small expense than the establishment of a small circulating library in every county . . . [1809 LETTER TO JOHN WYCHE]

★ I have now been thirty years availing myself of every possible opportunity of procuring Indian vocabularies to the same set of words . . . [1809 LETTER TO DR. BENJAMIN S. BARTON]

★ The learning of Greek and Latin, I am told, is going into disuse in Europe. I know not what their manners and occupations may call for: but it would be very ill-judged in us to follow their example in this instance. [NOTES ON THE STATE OF VIRGINIA, 1781]

★ Honesty is the first chapter in the Book of Wisdom. . . . Let it be our endeavor to merit the character of a just nation.

★ I never yet saw an instance of one of two disputants convincing the other by argument. I have seen many on their getting warm, becoming rude, and shooting one another. Conviction is the effect of our own dispassionate reasoning, either in solitude, or weighing within ourselves dispassionately what we hear from others standing uncommitted in argument ourselves. . . . When I hear another express an opinion, which is not mine, I say to myself, He has a right to his opinion, as I to mine; why should I question it. His error does me no injury . . . If a fact be misstated, it is probable he is gratified by a belief of it, and I have no right to deprive him of the gratification. If he wants information he will ask it, and then I will give it in measured terms; but if he still believes his own story, and shows a desire to dispute the fact with me, I hear him and say nothing. It is his affair, not mine, if he prefers error. [1808 LETTER TO THOMAS JEFFERSON RANDOLPH]

★ On American character:

In the North they are	In the South they are
cool	fiery
sober	Voluptuary
laborious	indolent
persevering	unsteady
independant	independant
Jealous of their own liberties, and just to those of others	zealous for their own liberties, but trampling on those of others
interested	generous
chicaning	candid
superstitious and hypocritical in their religion	without attachment or pretensions to any religion but that of the heart

These characteristics grow weaker and weaker by gradation from North to South and South to North, insomuch that an observing traveller, without the aid of the quadrant may always know his latitude by the character of the people among whom he finds himself. It is in Pennsylvania that the two characters seem to meet and blend and to form a people free from the extremes both of vice and virtue. Peculiar circumstances have given to New York the character which climate would have given had she been placed on the South instead of the North side of Pennsylvania. [1785 LETTER TO FRENCHMAN CHASTELLUX]

★ It is a part of the American character to consider nothing as desperate; to surmount every difficulty by resolution and contrivance.

★ The spirit of manufacture has taken deep root among us . . . [1809 LETTER TO P.S. DU-PONT DE NEMOURS]

★ Travelling . . . makes men wiser, but less happy. When men of sober age travel, they gather knowledge which they may apply use-fully for their country, but they are subject ever after to recollections mixed with regret, their affections are weakened by being ex-tended over more objects, and they learn new habits which cannot be gratified when they return home. Young men who travel are ex-posed to all these inconveniences in a higher degree . . . [1787 LETTER TO NEPHEW PETER CARR, AGE 15]

★ History, in general, only informs us what bad government is.

★ If the present [Continental] Congress errs in too much talking, how can it be otherwise, in a body to which the people send one hundred and fifty lawyers, whose trade it is to question everything, yield nothing, and talk by the hour? [AUTOBIOGRAPHY, 1821]

★ I think I knew General Washington intimately and thoroughly . . . His mind was great and powerful, without being of the first order; . . . no judgment was ever sounder. It was slow in operation, being little aided by invention or imagination, but sure in conclusion . . . He was incapable of fear, meeting personal dangers with the calmest unconcern. Perhaps the strongest feature in his character was prudence . . . He was . . . a wise, a good, and a great man. . . . His person, you know, was fine, his stature exactly what one would wish, his deportment easy, erect and noble; the best horseman of his age, and the most graceful figure that could be seen on horseback. [1814 LETTER TO DR. WALTER JONES]

★ A Tory has been properly defined to be a traitor in thought but not in deed.

★ In Great-Britain it is said their constitution relies on the house of commons for honesty, and the lords for wisdom; which would be a rational reliance if honesty were to be bought with money, and if wisdom were hereditary. [NOTES ON THE STATE OF VIRGINIA]

★ I fancy it must be the quantity of animal food eaten by the English which renders their character insusceptible of civilisation. I suspect it is in their kitchens and not in their churches that their reformation must be worked, and that Missionaries of that description from hence would avail more than those who should endeavor to tame them by precepts of religion or philosophy. [1785 LETTER FROM PARIS TO ABIGAIL ADAMS]

★ I have seen enough of political honors to know that they are but splendid torments. [1797 LETTER TO MARTHA JEFFERSON RANDOLPH]

★ This I hope will be the age of experiments in government, and that their basis will be founded on principles of honesty, not of mere force. [1796 LETTER TO JOHN ADAMS]

★ I have generally considered (one branch of the Federalists) rather as subjects for a mad-house. [1808 LETTER TO DR. THOMAS LEIB]

★ No occupation is so delightful to me as the culture of the earth, and no culture comparable to that of the garden. [1811 LETTER TO CHARLES WILSON PEALE]

★ My theory has always been, that if we are to dream, the flatteries of hope are as cheap, and pleasanter than the gloom of despair. [1817 LETTER TO FRANCOIS DE MARBOIS]

★ I steer my bark with Hope in the head, leaving Fear astern. [1816 LETTER TO JOHN ADAMS]

Jefferson's Legacy

Valedictory Words of Thos. Jefferson.

★ I carry with me the consolation of a firm persuasion that Heaven has in store for our beloved country long ages to come of prosperity and happiness. [EIGHTH ANNUAL MESSAGE TO CONGRESS, 1808]

★ My confidence in my countrymen generally leaves me without much fear for the future.

★ Of you, then, my neighbors, I may ask, in the face of the world, "whose ox have I taken, or whom have I defrauded? Whom have I oppressed, or of whose hand have I received a bribe to blind mine eyes therewith?" On your verdict I rest with conscious security. [ADDRESS TO THE INHABITANTS OF ALBEMARLE COUNTY IN VIRGINIA, 1809]

The third president of the United States, governor of Virginia, secretary of state and holder of many legislative offices wrote the following words to memorialize the actions for which he wished to be remembered:

Here was Buried
THOMAS JEFFERSON
Author of the
Declaration
of
American Independence
of the
Statute of Virginia
for
Religious Freedom
and Father of the
University of Virginia

These words appear on the gray granite obelisk marking his tomb in the family cemetery at Monticello.